An Artist's Journey
Down The Thames

JOHN DOYLE, RWS

An Artist's Journey Down The Thames

Foreword by John Ward, CBE, RA

PAVILION
MICHAEL JOSEPH

First published in Great Britain in 1988 by
PAVILION BOOKS LIMITED
196 Shaftesbury Avenue, London WC2H 8JL
in association with Michael Joseph Limited
27 Wrights Lane, Kensington, London W8 5TZ

Designed by Trevor Vincent

British Library Cataloguing in Publication Data

Doyle, John, 1928—
    An artist's journey down the Thames.
    I. England. Thames River.—Illustrations
    I. Title
    942.2'0858'0222

    ISBN 1-85145-267-2

Printed and bound in Italy by Arnoldo Mondadori

To my wife Elizabeth for all her patience and understanding

Contents

Foreword

It has been my pleasure to know John Doyle for nearly thirty years and from our earliest meetings I have admired his devotion to painting and drawing. 'It's a matter of character in the end,' my old friend Allan Gwynne Jones used to say and I suppose that what has always impressed me about John is the deep determination in his character to be a painter. Morsels of encouragement are always, as an act of courtesy, doled out to everyone who buys a box of paints but few persist beyond the first excitement of wagging a brushful of paint across paper or canvas. It needs small intelligence to see the lack of skills which first efforts display and, to acquire these skills, hours of practice are needed and the kind of application easy when young but much more difficult when older. The years I spent learning to draw in the lax atmosphere of an art school, John Doyle spent learning to become a foundry man in America.

Nowadays such work as these pictures of the Thames are not popular with those who write about art since they do not conform with what is in fashion at the moment. If fame and fortune had been John Doyle's ambition he may well have been better advised to follow the wilder paths of contemporary art but there is an obstinate honesty about his devotion to the job. His pictures make sense to himself. He is not forever looking over his shoulder for approval, for the patronizing nod from the art historian. Sturdily he turns a solid back on the squawking of such parasites as if saying, 'This I can do with all my heart, and all the skill of immense application, and I hope someone will take joy of my work.'

Here we have a feast. From my professional point of view an account of the painting of every picture would make good reading since those early days that John Doyle spent in the foundry were not wasted. His deftness in organizing so vast a project in the face of sullen English weather, the laws of trespass and other hazards of painting out of doors is formidable.

I grew up on the River Wye around Hereford, and I look back on days spent walking its banks, boating and swimming with deep gratitude for my good fortune. For those who know and love the Thames, John Doyle's book will be enjoyed as a record of the unique joys which a river can give. This I know is sheer lovely sentiment, but when there is the added bonus of skill and originality, achieved through a man's determination to be an artist, then indeed a book to treasure is created.

John Ward

Introduction

This is a book of my paintings and the story of their making. As such it is as unique as any personal statement must be. This is my excuse for adding yet another book to the hundreds that have appeared about our national river.

Julius Caesar is said to have christened the River Thames by naming the upper reaches 'Tamesis', meaning the beginning of life. Much controversy has arisen over the location of the source of the Thames. Officially it is at Thameshead, a few miles to the south-west of Cirencester. Its most serious rival is Seven Springs, where the Churn rises in the Cotswolds. Another possible source is the Swill Brook, rising to the south-west. There was also a man who claimed that the Thames rose in his cellar! I felt it my duty to settle the argument for myself by visiting both Thameshead and Seven Springs.

At Thameshead there is a slight depression in a quiet meadow with an ash tree leaning over a stone whose inscription proclaims that this is the source of the Thames. In front of it I found an inverted cone of pebbles disappearing into the ground, but of water, not a trace. As I visited the spot during one of the wettest summers of this century, I doubted whether I had come to the birthplace of the Thames, although I was told by an old man, who remembered Thameshead from his childhood, that the water used to spurt five feet into the air from this now miserable and dry pebbled hole.

Seven Springs lies high in the Cotswolds above Cheltenham. Here the water appears from seven cracks in the base of an old wall, and collects among stones and the odd beer can, trickling away through a pipe under the road to feed a duck pond on the other side. From there it runs dancing down its valley, past Cobberley to join its rival tributary near Cricklade.

I decided, on the evidence I found, that Seven Springs should bear the honour of the Thames' birthplace. After all, it is the furthest contender from the sea. But here I must leave the dispute; for does it really matter? I have felt free to roam with my paints and brushes in this lovely land that gives the Thames its birth.

At Lechlade the Thames becomes navigable. From here to Oxford she is the Isis, the country Thames, leisurely meandering through fields and farmland, under medieval bridges past Kelmscot, Buscot and Bablock Hythe.

Below Oxford, the tourist Thames begins and the cabin cruisers that line the banks and choke the backwaters stretch from here all the way to Teddington. Henley is the capital of the tourist Thames. Here the fine bridge carries two carved heads on the keystone of its central arch: Mother Isis, serene, calm and beautiful, looks back to the source while, on the eastern side, Father Thames, to whom she gives eternal birth, benign and godlike, gazes forever to the sea. The town itself is always bustling with life and seems to be waiting continually and with ever-mounting excitement for the next regatta.

Below Teddington, 'tide end town' where the tides begin, is, or was, the working Thames, the ancient witness to so much of the nation's past as she flows past Lambeth and Westminster, Whitehall and the Tower: palaces spiritual, temporal, administrative and authoritative. Snaking in ever-widening reaches, at last she joins the sea. Here in the estuary, where salt and fresh waters meet, marry and mingle, is a land of tides, saltings, the call of sea birds and waders, and the smell of mud; a lonely place in winter with vast skies and magnificent sunsets, so different from the crystal-clear water in the Cotswolds. I have painted it all, in all moods and weathers, out on the mud of the estuary in winter, enjoying the heat of summer upon its banks – always painting, for painting has become my life.

It helps enormously if one has a theme to work to when painting. Turner knew this and was at his happiest when travelling to collect material for his great series of watercolours: the Rhine, the Seine, the Loire, and the southern ports and watering places of England. Much of a landscape-painter's energy goes in searching and exploring and a theme limits the boundaries of the search. One quite literally has to go out and collect suitable subjects in the same way that people collect wild flowers or matchbox tops. It is nearly always the first impression that counts when painting and it is never easy to keep the first fresh image that inspired the picture clear in the mind. The more one looks into a subject, the more intriguing it becomes. But first comes the agony of choosing the place to paint it from. There is so much to consider, and the task is made no easier by the fact that rearranging nature is not easy. The time of day transforms a subject and even the simple problem of reaching the site cannot be ignored. All these things must be overcome before the pencil touches the paper.

I soon discovered that to explore a river it was necessary to have a boat. So many unspoilt stretches are inevitably far from roads and, where they are not, the riparian landlords have been forced to protect their property so securely that to reach the river proved nearly impossible. A boat brings with it the rights of a navigator and a freedom of movement denied to those on land. And so I bought the *Angela Jane*. She was not exactly elegant; in fact she was small and shabby and in need of a good coat of paint. The rain leaked into her dimunitive cabin which was only just large enough to shelter paints, paintings and painter from the vagaries of the weather. But she was fast and, after a bit of practice, I found that she was easy to handle.

I had to learn the ways of life on water. Tying knots and keeping anchor chains and ropes neatly in their right places was difficult – they always seemed to get into a tangle. Then there were the locks to negotiate; not too difficult if the lock-keeper was on duty, but a dreadful sweat if he had gone home. Anchoring in mid-stream, in a high wind, in exactly the same place for several days at a stretch was one of the more difficult tasks. In the end the *Angela Jane* enabled me to explore all along the Thames and to discover views hidden from the eyes of those on land. Indeed she became a very useful floating studio. I thought of Monet on the Seine!

I cannot summon the necessary momentum needed to carry a painting through from start to finish by sitting in a warm studio or by poring over the finest photographs. My imagination can blossom only in front of the subject. I need the stimulation of changing light, atmosphere and incident before me. If it is cold, I need to shiver a little; if it is hot, to share in the heat; if wet, I need at least to be aware of the damp and, if windy, to feel the wind upon my face. I need cats, dogs, sheep, cattle, birds and people; I need clouds flying, water rippling, light catching leaves blown by the wind. In short, I need pulsing, throbbing life all around me, even if these things do not always find their way into my pictures.

I love to talk to people while I paint and to share my experiences with them. In this I am at odds with many of my fellow painters who generally prefer to work in peace. For me, painting is seeing. There is no conscious mental effort, no careful and detailed planning, little contriving – only an inexplicable feeling that tells me when I am right or wrong. The visual impressions fall on the retina and flow subconsciously down the arm, through the fingertips and, via the brush or pencil, they arrive on the paper. Like a top-class tennis player, one has to perform instinctively without being aware of the mechanical processes involved. All I can do is try to copy nature faithfully in the belief that nature is generally right: twig by twig, brick by brick, each leaf, every ripple in the water. If this produces fussiness, it must be muted and, if it is too loose, the structure must be strengthened. It is only when a painter is satisfied that he can lay down his brush and, because a true painter is never satisfied, a painting is never really finished. One is reminded of Whistler's remark in court during his libel action against Ruskin. When asked if the picture was finished, he replied, 'I don't intend to do any more to it'.

Painting out of doors brings endless problems. I sometimes long for the imagination and visual memory of Turner which would enable me to re-create a whole changing scene with nothing but the aid of a slight pencil sketch, while sitting in a warm studio on a cold December day. But Turner was a genius and could create his beautiful essays of colour from his mind. They were never copies of nature, but great magical visions that remind one of the fundamental truth of nature.

People who have never tried to paint probably do not realise that one cannot sit in the same place all day long with the light continually changing with the sun's motion. The shadows and mood of the morning can create indecipherable chaos by the afternoon. One has to return to exactly the same spot at the same time, day after day, until the painting is finished.

Time is more precious to a landscape painter than to most people. Even at twenty a painter can only expect to see fifty winters, fifty summers; it is never enough and, as the years pass and skill improves, so the pressure of passing time increases. Therefore, to make sure that no precious moment is wasted, several pictures must be worked on over the same period. A painting for sunrise, another for morning, and so on through the day until the fading light forces one to stop. Then there are subjects for dull days which, because there are no shadows, have the advantage that one can remain working on the same picture hour after hour in the constant diffused light. Sometimes a fine morning is followed by a cloudy afternoon. Many times I have listened to the weatherman and landed in the wrong place, only to find on moving that the weather has changed too and the day is spent in two wrong locations. When this happens, the only answer is to draw or to give up and explore.

The problem does not end here – there are the seasons to consider. These can sometimes overtake a painting. In spring, the subject becomes more obscured by new green leaves every day, while summer, with its long days, can be exhausting as I sometimes have as many as eight paintings on the go at once. Winter is more leisurely and does not demand unsocial hours. The shadows are longer, the tones richer. The reverse of spring happens in autumn when the beautiful golden leaves fade and drop before one's eyes; if the painting is not finished then it must be put away in a drawer until next year makes it possible to re-create the transient mood that first inspired its conception. There are also winter paintings of snow, of mists and a thousand different changes in the weather. If these cannot be completed in one mad dash, they too must be relegated to the waiting drawer. Sometimes they fall by the wayside because, when one returns to continue them, a housing estate has appeared in the meadow one was painting or the building that had formed the central feature of a composition has been demolished. Thus it is that a landscape painter has many things to think about at the same time and it is not easy to keep them all under control.

I would not change my method of working even if I could because for me, nature is never boring. Nature never repeats herself and, in following her, one can forget the obsession with a personal originality that so often seems to blight the vision of fine painters today. Like two finger prints, no two trees, no two blades of grass, no two sunsets were ever, or will ever be, the same. And so I never find this frenzied copying tedious. Indeed, by going on and on, something at last seems to happen to the paper on which I am working: suddenly it seems to ripen. I am reminded of these lines of poetry which I can recall from somewhere:

> *Give me a young man's frenzy,*
> *And I'll myself remake,*
> *Till I am Timon or Lear,*
> *Or that old William Blake,*
> *Who bangs his head against a wall,*
> *Till time itself obeys his call.*

It is only by the constant banging of the head against a wall that this ripening of the paper's surface can be achieved. For me there is no such thing as overworking a painting. Indeed, there can be few of my pictures that I could not improve. I have found that freshness and spontaneity do not have to be so in fact, only to appear so in effect. It is not the painting that tires but the painter – scratching, sponging, cutting off bits here, adding new pieces there, fingers, thumbs, chalk, pencils, gum, even washes of cold tea – anything can be used to bring the artist's ideas to fruition. It is impossible to explain how this is done since I scarcely know myself. I do know that talent is not such an uncommon commodity as is generally supposed and a little can be made to go far; but

the passion that forces a painter out of his bed on a cold winter morning to sit in the snow as the washes freeze on the paper, is the madness that is needed and is more rare.

My journey down the Thames has taken a year and all the pictures were painted on the spot. Sadly many fine views and famous places have had to be passed over; but if some of the joy and wonder I have felt in my love affair with this river is passed on through these pictures then I will feel that it has all been worthwhile.

John Doyle

The Paintings

1

Ashton Keynes

Although I have sided with Seven Springs against Thameshead as the source of the Thames, I found the upper reaches of the Isis more paintable and so abandoned the Churn with regret.

Ashton Keynes is only a few miles down river from Thameshead. It is a very pretty village with the river running straight through the middle. The surrounding countryside has been ruined by gravel extraction which has turned the water meadows into hundreds of lakes known as the Cotswold Water Park. An elderly local inhabitant showed me a book of photographs of the village and Thames at the turn of the century. Then the countryside was breathtakingly beautiful with unspoilt sand-covered roads and magnificent elm trees. A hundred years later the contrast is horrifying. These old photographs reveal the havoc and destruction that we have wrought on our countryside – alas it is still going on.

John Doyle

2

Lechlade from St John's Lock

At Lechlade, a delightful little market town, the Thames becomes navigable and the first boatyard on the river caters to the needs of the holiday-maker.

I painted this from St John's Lock, the first lock on the Thames. The locks from here to Godstow, just above Oxford, are manual and look more attractive than those that have been electrified. The statue of Father Thames that reclines by the lockside used to be at Thameshead but it was moved here a few years ago for safekeeping.

3

Buscot

I painted this picture on three mild January afternoons. The first two were sunny and I was dazzled by the setting sun and could only put in the black shapes against the light. On the third afternoon it was misty and I was able to finish the detail keeping the memory of the brilliant light always in my mind.

I love painting trees in winter. It is a fact that branches and trunks do not taper; they diminish each time they divide, the combined area of the branches being equal in area to the main stem from which they sprang. In other words the area of all the twigs added together is equal to the cross-sectional area of the tree's trunk. This wonderfully neat law of growth is mentioned by Ruskin in *Modern Painters* and I know it to be true from direct observation.

The church has two windows by Sir Edward Coley Burne-Jones and some painted panels attributed to Andrea Mantegna. There are also carpets and curtains designed by William Morris who lived a few miles downstream at Kelmscott.

John Doyle.

4

Swinford Bridge

Swinford's toll bridge was built by the Earl of Abingdon in 1769 to replace the ferry that had been here from earliest times. His descendant collected the tolls until 1981 when it was sold to a new owner.

The composition created problems although I was determined to paint this view. There was an unsatisfactory void in the foreground. Sheep arrived and claimed a place in the field but this, although it helped, did not solve the problem. The glancing light on the bridge and the colours of early morning were just as I could have wished but I could not decide what to put at the bottom of the picture. Just before deciding to give up, I went to my vantage point an hour earlier. It was a fine, bright morning and the shadows streaming across the grass did the trick. Sometimes one can make a painting more exciting by using changing light. I painted the light here over a period of several hours on purpose. The shadows in the foreground were painted early in the morning and the glancing light on the bridge did not reach it until two hours later.

5

The Trout, Wolvercote

This is a fine old pub, so much a part of the landscape that it seems to grow out of the soil on which it is built.

I painted this picture in late autumn and the difference in the view between the day I began and the day on which I finished was considerable. I could not work on the picture for nearly a week because the sun was sulking and when I managed to get back to it, many leaves had fallen. I only just made it.

6

Oxford from Godstow

This is a wide-angle view across Port Meadow with Oxford on the skyline. I have said I seldom contrive but in this case I have. From where I was sitting the wonderful skyline that made me choose this view was, in fact, obscured by the trees in the middle distance. By shifting my position to the left, by several hundred yards, I was able to draw the distant spires of Oxford and, at the same time, by returning to my original position beside the lock, include the great sweep of the river as it turns towards Godstow.

This is not cheating if the painting is better for such tactics, and many old prints show this view before the trees had grown.

This is a view of the Thames where I longed to see the mast of a river barge but there are limits to what can be done without becoming phoney – the eventual outcome of such a course would be to put in stage coaches.

7

All Souls College, Oxford

On the opposite side of the Radcliffe Camera from Brasenose lies All Souls. It was founded by Henry Chichele, Archbishop of Canterbury, who had been one of the original scholars to enter William of Wykeham's New College. He founded All Souls in 1438, twenty-three years after the battle of Agincourt as a memorial 'for all souls . . . who fell in the wars for the Crown of France'.

Chichele followed the plans of William of Wykeham closely and the small quadrangle bordering the High Street remains much the same as it did in the year of its completion in 1443. The college was founded for a warden and forty fellows and did not exceed this number until this century. It is the only Oxford college that does not admit undergraduate or graduate students. The distinction of membership is reserved for scholars elected by examination, research fellows, holders of professorial chairs and for people who have achieved eminence and distinction in some special field of learning.

The great quadrangle shown here was designed by Nicholas Hawksmoor around the Codrington Library that stretches along the whole of the north side. Probably to keep his new design in sympathy with the medieval buildings on the south side, Hawksmoor returned to the Gothic tradition, long discontinued by his time, and he thereby preceded the Gothic revival by half a century. This view was painted from the north-east corner of the quadrangle looking west.

8

The Radcliffe Camera from Brasenose College, Oxford

Turner painted this view in his youth for a series for the *Oxford Almanack*. Maybe it was cheek on my part even to try it. However, no sooner does one start to paint than all the complexities of the subject completely absorb one's concentration and such things are forgotten. This is one of those fine ready-made compositions that architecture so often presents to the painter.

When this drawing was finished I looked at it in a mirror which is always a good way to check one's work. To my horror, I found the perspective of the elipse on the Radcliffe Camera was out and the tower above the gateway was falling over. This had to be corrected and, by placing a fresh piece of paper under the drawing, I was able to cut out the mistake. The new piece was then inserted and the drawing re-done. If one cuts along a line in the composition, it is almost impossible to see the cut unless one knows where to look for it.

9

Radley College Chapel

The manor of Radley, once belonging to Abingdon Abbey, is five miles from Oxford. In 1847 Radley Hall was leased to the Reverend William Sewell and the Reverend Robert Singleton who founded a boys' public school. The school flourished and is now one of the leading public schools in England with 600 boys.

Radley has always had a great rowing tradition being situated so close to the Thames. I kept the *Angela Jane* in the boathouse while painting this picture of the chapel which was designed in 1895 by Sir Thomas Jackson. I chose this subject because the sunlight on the red brick contrasting with the green of the leaves produced a magical effect and the apples on the trees and on the ground brilliantly echoed the red of the chapel. The contrast between the animate and inanimate is always exciting and buildings seen through trees produce natural abstract shapes. I find it is better to search for the abstract in reality rather than create it in the mind.

10

Abingdon Mead

I rounded a bend in the river and saw the spire of Abingdon Church rising out of the meadows, so I anchored and painted this fine view.

The fine perpendicular church of St Helen's, whose width exceeds its length, has a charming triangular churchyard surrounded by superb almshouses, some built as early as 1446.

11

Abingdon

Abingdon is one of the finest Thamesside towns and also one of the oldest, having been a prosperous market town for at least 900 years. Until 1974 it was the county town of Berkshire and the County Hall, built by Christopher Kempster, one of Wren's masons on St Paul's Cathedral, still dominates the market-place.

The painting of the river frontage depends on reflections for its effect. In completely still water a mirror image would be reflected but, of course, this very rarely happens as the water is continually stirred by the wind. Only the vertical lines can be seen clearly because horizontal features, instead of being repeated on successive waves, are only reflected on a few. Clear water, like a mirror, cannot receive a shadow because the light is reflected off it but, as this picture shows, river water is seldom clear and therefore shadows fall freely across the surface.

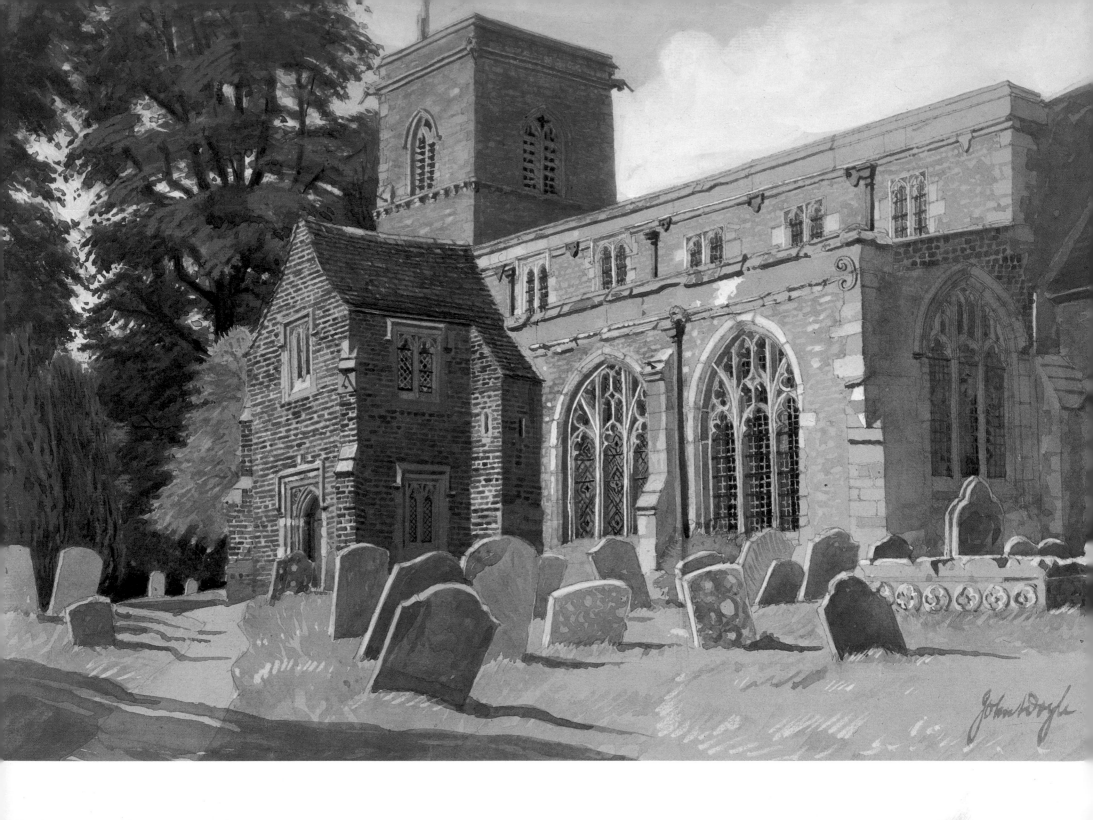

12

Sutton Courtenay Church

If I had to choose between saving a painting or a beautiful building, I would choose the building. Of all the arts, architecture must be the most accomplished. How rare really fine architecture is and how lovely it becomes when adorned by the hand of nature: lichen on stone, rust on iron, weathering on brickwork. Many of England's parish churches are perfect examples of this and, like the fourteenth-century church of All Saints that I have painted here, they are often magnificent works of art in their own right.

Herbert Asquith, the first Earl of Oxford, and Eric Blair, better known to the world as George Orwell, lie buried in the churchyard here.

13

Sunset at Appleford

At Appleford I chose to paint just after the sun had disappeared below the horizon and the skyline stood out against the dying light like a black paper cut-out. I was surprised that the red sky was not reflected in the water but there was a stiffish breeze blowing and this may have ruffled the water so that it only reflected the light directly above it.

14

Moonrise, Long Wittenham

I once read that Van Gogh went painting by moonlight with candles stuck in his hat and I dismissed it as a fairy tale. I have painted quite a few moonlight pictures and now know that this must have been quite true. The only way to paint at night is to tie a lamp to your hat – no other method works. If you put a lamp on a pole your vision is immediately imprisoned in a cone of light and you have to turn it out to see, then on again to draw, very disturbing and impractical. With the lamp on your hat it becomes as easy as painting by day for when one raises one's head, the light is dissipated into the night and when one lowers it, the light shines clearly on the paper. I have found that this procedure arouses quite a bit of curiosity if there happen to be people about!

15

Clifton Hampden Bridge

I painted this fine brick bridge early in the morning, catching the slanting light of the rising sun. Sir George Gilbert Scott, grandfather of the architect who designed Battersea power station, built the bridge, restored the church of St Michael and All Angels – alas, nearly to extinction – and the manor house behind the trees in the background. The Barley Mow Inn on the extreme right of the picture is where Jerome K. Jerome is supposed to have written part of *Three Men in a Boat*.

16

Day's Lock

Day's Lock is situated at the end of the village of Little Wittenham which nestles under Castle Hill. The hill is topped with an iron-age fort and the famous group of trees known as Wittenham Clumps.

The sunset here was painted with the 'one mad dash' approach. Some effects of light such as sunrise, sunset or even a rainbow, change so quickly that one only has seconds in which to capture the fleeting effect. When the watercolour dried and I had taken the painting home to my studio in Kent, it seemed so weak that I almost abandoned it. However, I was pleased with the idea and composition, so I salvaged the picture with pastels. Although lacking in detail and delicacy, the whole painting gains force from the dark, massed shapes set against the light of the dying sun.

17

Dorchester Abbey

The Romans built their town of Durocina here in a bend of the Thames though the little town is, in fact, on a tributary called the Thame. St Birinus was sent from Rome to continue the conversion of the Saxons started by St Augustine some thirty-five years before. As he journeyed up the Thames, the inhabitants came to hear him preach, and because they gathered on both banks, churches were built opposite each other as at Windsor and Eton, Hurley and Medmenham, Pangbourne and Whitchurch. He founded this great abbey in 634.

Most of the Abbey was destroyed at the dissolution in 1536 but the Abbey Church survived. It is one of the best in England with a particularly beautiful fourteenth-century choir. There are many treasures here including a superb Jesse window and one of the finest Norman lead fonts in England.

18

Sunset near Pangbourne

The Thames near Pangbourne is the world of Mole and Ratty and Mr Toad. Kenneth Grahame lived in Pangbourne and this stretch of the river became the setting for *The Wind in the Willows*. The sun is going down over the wild woods and reflecting off the water – one of the most difficult natural effects to paint successfully.

19

The Mill, Mapledurham

The mill at Mapledurham is mentioned in the *Domesday Book*: 'William de Warrene holds Mapledurham of the King . . . there is a mill worth 20 shillings and 10 acres of meadow.' The present mill looks much the same as it would have done in the late eighteenth century although you can still trace the medieval mill through its timbers, walls and roof trusses which form the centre of the building. Many of the old mills on the Thames have disappeared completely and are only remembered by the weirs and locks that the mediaeval millers built to power their wheels. The mill here has been restored by its present owner and is the only working mill left on the Thames.

I painted this picture from my dinghy in the fading afternoon light of late September. Painting from a dinghy is a devilish job. The boat bobs about at the slightest ripple and, unless moored securely, swings round in the wind, totally changing the perspective.

20

Mapledurham

Although there has been a manor here since the Norman Conquest, the present Elizabethan house was built by Sir Michael Blount in 1588 and it has belonged to his ancestors ever since.

The eighteenth-century poet Alexander Pope used to visit to court Teresa and Martha, the daughters of Lyster Blount. He quarrelled with Teresa but his friendship with Martha lasted until his death in 1744.

The Thames runs right beside the house in the middle distance. One of the gables facing the Thames is covered with oyster shells. This was a sign to Catholics fleeing down the Thames from persecution during the Reformation that here they would find help.

21

Henley

It was in Henley that I bought the *Angela Jane* and a small dingy for exploring all those places that other boats couldn't reach. On the first day I tied up on the bank to look at Temple Island and a man in the next boat gave me champagne in a tea cup. It was a good start to the nautical part of my Thames journey. The dinghy was hellish to handle and I had to use it to reach the island from which this picture was painted. I sat on my stool on the roots of a chestnut tree covered in birds' droppings – mainly coots' with the odd goose's and crested diver's thrown in for good measure. On the second day I stood on the wrong end of the dinghy and it did a cartwheel, landing me in the river – I suppose I had to be baptised sometime.

The picture itself was difficult because I did not like the ugly cabin cruisers and I nearly gave it up. In the end I turned to my pastels and the picture seemed to come to life again. I have described the magnificent bridge in the Introduction.

22

Regatta Reach, Henley

I was in my boat on this stretch of water when I learned never to go too near an oarsman, to keep to the right and not to go faster than walking pace. What the rather elderly man from the Leander Club against whom I committed all these misdemeanours actually said, I do not intend to repeat.

I was rather pleased with this painting. I must confess to never really liking the colour green until I made this journey but had I not painted trees in full leaf I would have had nothing left to paint. Velázquez said that one should look for the greys in a colour and for colours in grey – this principle certainly applies to green. No other colour seems to have more tints or hues.

23

Temple Island, Henley

This charming little temple was designed by Thomas Wyatt as a folly for the owners of nearby Fawley Court. It has fine frescoes inside and is the starting point for races up river to Henley. The Henley Regatta committee recently bought the island and its temple.

The painting was done on my thin Ingres paper that I find so sensitive to use, especially when using body-colour as I have done here. To preserve the paintings and to stop the thin paper from crinkling, I stick them down on acid-free mounting board with conservation paste. Cheap card or hardboard made from woodpulp contains acid and this in time will spread into the picture breaking down the structure of the paper making it brittle and discoloured. This is called foxing and is difficult to remove.

24

Culham Court

I passed this beautiful Georgian house on my way up the Thames from Marlow to Henley on a late July evening. The sun was making the red bricks glow and it looked the epitome of an English country house. I called on its owner who very kindly allowed me to sit on his terrace and paint. The figure in front of the house is a fine piece of sculpture by Elizabeth Frink known as *The Striding Madonna*. There is another in Salisbury Cathedral Close but I think she looks better here.

To get both the house and the river into the painting I had to compress the garden and trees in the middle; even then there was a danger of creating two pictures that would scream to be cut in half. To weld the two halves together I lengthened the shadows into the meadow on the left and carried the green of the distant hills right across the picture.

John Doyle

25

Harleyford Manor

This charming red brick mansion was built by Sir Robert Taylor in 1765. It has recently been restored and looks magnificent with its lawns running down to the river. Alas, it is surrounded by an ugly marina and I conveniently left out the motor cruisers moored along the bank beneath it.

The reason for choosing this subject, though the house itself was reason enough, was the exciting contrast between the red brick in the midday sun and the myriad shades of green all around it.

26

Bisham

Bisham is about a mile downstream from Marlow. All Saints Church is seen on the far bank and the abbey, now the sports centre of the Central Council of Physical Recreation, is further downstream behind the trees of its park. It was originally owned by the Knights Templar but, when the order was suppressed in the fourteenth century, William Montacute, Earl of Salisbury, founded an Augustinian priory here in its place. Temple Lock, just beyond the limits of the picture, is a reminder of its earlier history.

The tree on the right was a problem: put all the leaves in and it would distract from the church; paint it too broadly without enough depth and it would look insubstantial and unreal – trial and error is the only way to solve the dilemma.

27

Marlow Lock

The constant light and lack of shadows that I experienced at Marlow Lock enabled me to work all day without having to move to another picture.

The subject is complicated and had to be drawn in great detail before painting started. Having drawn a very rough outline, I started at the top of the paper, with the apex of the church spire, to produce a detailed skeleton. The human eye can measure vertically and horizontally with incredible accuracy but it is not so good along a curve or along a line at an angle. It is possible to train the eye by imagining – or even drawing – a fine grid on the paper. Any outline drawing will slowly disappear as the paint takes over, but without a framework, the whole picture would fall to pieces.

28

Windsor Castle from Salt Hill

To paint this view I actually sat on the edge of the embankment that carries the new trunk road across the Thames at this point. It was late autumn and the sun catching the autumn colours was quite magnificent. Again this was a fleeting moment and I had to catch as much as I could quickly.

Founded by William the Conqueror, Windsor Castle has been the principal home of the Kings and Queens of England for nearly a thousand years. Its history is well known and can be found elsewhere.

29

Windsor Castle from Eton College

I sat in the field in front of the college to paint this winter picture of Windsor Castle. I love the subtlety of the colours in winter and find them more stimulating than the bright greens of summer.

30

Windsor Castle under snow

This was painted about a mile further upstream from the previous picture. I particularly enjoy painting snow (although keeping warm can be a problem) and find that the winter colours are even more exciting when contrasted with white.

31

Eton College and Chapel

The young King Henry VI had been greatly impressed by William of Wykeham's College at Winchester when he decided to use it as a model when founding Eton in 1440. Both colleges were founded to teach seventy poor scholars and Henry even took the headmaster of Winchester to Eton to start his college. The chapel, seen here in the sunshine of an October afternoon, is one of the finest in England. King's College, Cambridge, founded by Henry at the same time, has a similar chapel that is probably the most splendid perpendicular building in England.

The octagonal college kitchen with its great pointed roof is still in use, though greatly modernised. Behind it is the roof of college hall where the scholars dine and the two cupolas are on the top of Lupton's Tower, built in 1520 and named after a Provost of that name. The seventy scholars still live in college, educated either wholly or in part by the foundation. The school that grew up round the college now consists of 1,200 boys and, being situated like Radley near the banks of the Thames, it has a long and creditable rowing tradition.

Eton College from Romney's Lock

When I painted this picture of Eton from Romney's Island looking across the river, the sun was setting just behind the trees on the right and making the red brick of the College buildings glow red. The plane tree in front of the chapel was just coming into leaf; another day and the chapel would have been hidden from here. The whole painting is based on the late evening light and had to be done quickly. It was possible to get the drawing done earlier in the evening but the moment of truth with a subject like this lasts for no more than fifteen to twenty minutes.

Eton College from the Masters' Boathouse (morning)

This and the following picture of my favourite view on the Thames were painted on the same day. They show how a place can change its character completely in different lights.

Reflections form an important part of both pictures. The reflections on the ripples create a whole multitude of little images which dance toward our feet, enlongating the objects reflected from the far bank. In perfectly clear water both object and image would be of the same length.

34

Eton College from the Masters' Boathouse (Evening)

The Masters' Boathouse, in front of which I sat to paint this picture, is the home of the Eton rowing eights and it is along this stretch of the Thames that they train for competition in the summer regattas. This is also the boathouse from which the famous procession of boats takes place on the Fourth of June.

John Doyle.

35

Petersham House

Petersham village nestles under Richmond Hill. It must be the grandest village in England for it contains more mansions than any other I know – at least six houses of stately home proportions. Petersham House is an excellent example. In the churchyard lies Captain Vancouver, founder of the city that bears his name.

36

Syon House

Built on the site of a fourteenth-century monastery founded by Henry V, the present house is mainly fifteenth-century although it was refaced in 1825. It has a magnificent interior designed in 1761 by Robert Adam, who worked on Osterley Park for the banker Robert Childe at about the same time. A heronry has existed on this site from medieval times.

The painting was done on my usual brown Ingres paper that lends itself particularly well to the colours of mid-winter.

37

Strand-on-the-Green

It would be hard to find a lovelier walk than the tow path that leads down river from Kew Bridge. Tight up against the path are some of the prettiest small Georgian houses in London. John Zoffany RA lived along here from 1780 to 1810 and when I dined in one of the houses recently, the view of the river with no cars in sight gave me a sense of what the world must have been like over a hundred years ago.

I painted this picture just before the arrival of the spring foliage which would have obscured the houses. I heightened the dock leaves in the foreground with pastels when I had finished with the watercolours. The matt pastel brings an extra kick to the picture if it is done with sensitivity but one has to be careful that the lines are not too crude or they are inclined to disturb the eye.

38

Temple, Chiswick Park

The third Earl of Burlington was an amateur architect of exceptional ability. His house at Chiswick is a little Palladian masterpiece. It was designed for parties and has no bedrooms. One can picture the guests arriving in their coaches to while away the night in the grounds and temples, such as the one shown here, then returning back to their own mansions in the dawn.

39

Hammersmith Terrace

I love mud. It is not perhaps suitable for a picnic but lovely to paint – it reflects the sky and is a maze of little runnels of water that make beautiful natural patterns that are quite beyond any contriving.

This is a fine terrace of Georgian houses. A. P. Herbert lived in the second house from the end. Chiswick must have been lovely and peaceful before the Cromwell Road extension brought the roar of traffic to within a few yards of its church, seen here in the distance. Hogarth had his country weekend cottage a few hundred yards from the river and it is the setting for much of Thackeray's *Vanity Fair*. How sad it is that, with all our ingenuity, we cannot plan our affairs so that such places are not ruined!

40

The Chelsea Physic Garden

The Apothecaries founded this garden for the study of plants in 1673. The Botanic Gardens at Oxford were founded in 1621 for the same purpose. They chose their site on the banks of the Thames at Chelsea, already rich in gardens of the great houses. Many of the trees were brought here by river, for the steps led from the water gate straight down to the river until the building of the Embankment in 1874.

The statue is that of Sir Hans Sloane, who saved the garden from decline in the early years of the eighteenth century. He had bought the manor of Chelsea from Lord Cheyne in 1712 and then granted the Apothecaries a lease in perpetuity.

I started this painting in August and worked on it intermittently through the summer. By mid-October it was nearly finished when the disastrous hurricane of 16 October 1987 almost destroyed the garden. The catalpa on the right of the picture survived but it was impossible to finish the painting except from memory. I decided to leave the painting unfinished, not only because I felt that I had said all that needed saying but also because I wanted it to be a reminder of that dreadful night of destruction.

41

Westminster from Waterloo Bridge

Sometimes the difficulties confronting the execution of a picture seem insurmountable and yet the very surmounting of them becomes the reason for its success. Everything that could go wrong, went wrong here. I had to carry the picture a long way – Waterloo Bridge is not an ideal place to park. The weather had to be overcast to get the effect that the subject seemed to demand. This meant that at some time during the painting's execution it had to rain and Waterloo Bridge offers no shelter. The traffic was distracting and the wind shook the side of a packing case that I used for a drawing board, blowing all the dust, grit and refuse of several hundred yards of pavement into my eyes, my water and my paint box. One can stand quite a low temperature in still air but the wind factor makes even a mild day miserable. Somehow this wide romantic stretch of water was captured on the paper. It was one of Monet's favourite views of London.

42

Tower Bridge from Rotherhithe

A rather grey and misty afternoon faced me when I came to paint this famous view from Rotherhithe. I had to paint it very quickly because the effect of the setting sun through mist is so transient. Luckily the paper remained quite wet while it was being painted. I used one of my favourite biscuit-coloured Ingres papers made by the Zirkall Mill in the Black Forest. This paper is slightly absorbent and, in the misty atmosphere prevalent that day, the paper stayed damp. On a hot dry day the paper can be kept damp by putting blotting paper under the top sheet. With the paper slightly wet it is possible to recreate the mistiness of the view more easily.

43

Rotherhithe

The little white building on the Wapping bank is The Prospect of Whitby, the pub beloved by Whistler, and in Rotherhithe Parish Church behind the old warehouses on the right, the captain of the *Mayflower* lies buried.

Like the view of Deptford on the next page, Rotherhithe was painted on two sheets of whatman paper. This beautiful handmade paper is, alas, no longer available. I stained the paper with cold tea as I also did for the painting of the Naval College at Greenwich. This deadens the white of the paper and makes it receptive to body-colour, white on white paper brings problems. The tea gives a beautiful even tone to the surface and is a joy to work on. It has the added advantage that it can be scratched down to the white paper again where this is needed.

44

Deptford and Limehouse Reach

This is certainly the largest watercolour I have ever painted and must be one of the largest ever to be painted entirely in the open. The scene was so grand that, like the previous picture, it demanded more and more space as it proceeded. Eventually I had to join two sheets of elephant whatman paper together to complete it. The two sheets are cut together so they fit following the lines of the drawing so that the join does not show. I used quite a lot of pastel in this picture. Pastels go very well with watercolour and bring a brilliance and depth to the picture that is, perhaps, nearer to oil painting than traditional watercolour. This tendency is highlighted even further by mixing white with the watercolour paint. This is called body-colour. Watercolours are transparent; pastels and body-colour are opaque. Striking effects can be achieved by combining these two opposing qualities.

45

The Royal Naval College, Greenwich

Here is what must be one of the grandest views on the Thames and I only hope I have done it justice. The painting is about five feet wide and its creation caused me more problems than any other on the journey. Firstly, the panorama was so vast that it had to be narrowed down into limits that made visual sense. I knew that I could make a fair representation of John Flamsteed's old observatory and that as a result the view of London and St Paul's would go into the distant mist and golden light where it belonged. This meant a whole line of trees had to be cut out to get the Queen's House into the centre. There were several days of scribbling and erasing before a pencil ghost of a possible picture appeared. Then, with a wash of cold tea and the highlights rubbed in, the picture was off to a good start. The sky and distance did not present too much trouble but the buildings of the College in the middle distance did. If they were too finely finished, they carried no weight when one stood back from the picture; if the detail was suppressed too much, the structure started to disintegrate and become unconvincing. In the end paintings like this become battles of trial and error and they have to be broadened and refined alternately until a balance is struck.

46

Croom's Hill, Blackheath

The houses round Blackheath were built by the more wealthy citizens of London fleeing from the plague; Blackheath and Hampstead each have a 'Vale of Health'. General Wolfe, who led the British capture of Quebec, lived with his parents overlooking the park and just behind the spot where I sat to do this painting is the Ranger's House, once the residence of the fourth Earl of Chesterfield, where many of the famous letters to his son were written.

I enjoy painting all things architectural. I particularly love painting bricks and London is wonderfully rich in bricks baked from the clay on which it is built.

47

The Royal Observatory, Greenwich Park

Charles II commissioned Sir Christopher Wren to design the first observatory on the hill behind his palace at Greenwich 'for the observator's habitation and a little pompe'. The Royal warrant makes clear that the purpose of the building was 'in order to the finding out of longitude of places and perfecting navigation and astronomy'.

The Reverend John Flamsteed was the first Astronomer Royal and his successors lived here until 1939. The Royal Observatory is now housed in Herstmonceux in Sussex and the original buildings have been turned into a fine museum that tells the history of Charles II's far-sighted aims.

The Greenwich meridian passes to the east of the Observatory, close to the original clock that kept Greenwich Mean Time. This clock was geared to the crimson ball on the mast above the Observatory and the ball still drops daily at precisely 1 p.m. as it has done since 1837. This time signal was installed so that ships in the river below could adjust their chronometers before starting out on voyages all over the world

48

Tilbury

The working Thames once extended as far as navigation was possible up the river. As roads improved and the railways provided a faster and cheaper method of transport than water, so the traffic on the Thames slowly died. Now the working Thames starts here and although I long for the sail or mast of a barge, the ships and small boats are still thrilling to draw.

49

Gravesend

I remember as a child seeing ships by their hundred lining the River Thames from the pool, downstream as far as one could see. Now this may seem a rather bleak and ugly world although I found a fascination in it born from just these dreary qualities.

50

Whitstable

Whitstable lies at the eastern end of the Swale, the channel separating Sheppey from the rest of Kent. Sunsets are particularly fine in the flat wastes of the Thames Estuary. Perhaps this is a result of the dust and fumes carried on the prevailing wind from London, refracting the rays of the sinking sun.

In Roman times Whitstable was famous for its oysters and they are still gathered in the beds that lie under the water in the middle of the picture. They are best in September and October and, now that the Thames is slowly recovering from the pollution that has spoilt it for the past hundred years, they are on the increase once more. Painted looking up the estuary, this last picture seems very far away from the shining trickles of water I found in the Cotswolds where my journey began.

Acknowledgements

I would like to thank the following people for all their help and advice in producing this book:

Gillian Catto of the Catto Gallery whose idea it was that I should do this book and without whose help it would never have seen the light of day; Mr John Ward, CBE, RA, for writing the Foreword and for teaching me how to paint; the Rt Hon. Sir Patrick Nairne, GCB, MC, for kindly checking my introduction; Mr and Mrs Michael Behrens for allowing me to paint Culham Court and Mr John and Lady Anne Eyston for allowing me to paint Maple-durham; Mr Hugh Kelly who photographed the original paintings.

I am also grateful to those people who allowed me to reproduce paintings in their possession including Mrs I. M. Harvey, Mr Raymond Parry, Mr Anthony Wilson, the Council and Warden of Radley College and the Society of Apothecaries.

Finally, I would like to thank all the lock-keepers, landladies and kind friends I met on the Thames who gave me their help and encouragement.

John Doyle